The Play Paradigm

How to Transform Your Life Through the Power of Play

Rory M-J

Dear Dan,
Best Wishes
Rory M-J

DEDICATION

To Vincent.

TABLE OF CONTENTS

ABOUT THE AUTHOR

Rory James MacLaren-Jackson ('Rory M-J') is a UK-based Elite Coach and Clinical Hypnotherapist with specialist insight into personal development, human communication and behavioural change.

For online products and services:
rorymj.com

For 1-2-1 sessions, workshops & consultancy services:
unlockingchange.com

1.
INTRODUCTION

This short book is designed to prompt a shift in mindset and provide you with practical steps to improve your relationship with the powerful, transformational state of 'play'.

Over the years, play has emerged as one of the most important concepts in my positive change work, whether I'm working with individuals in a therapeutic or coaching context or helping organisations.

My perspective as a hypnotist and mindset specialist also gives me a particular insight into the nature and power of play that, I'll go as far to suggest, makes this book a must-read for almost anyone.

It is rare for me to meet someone whose life and outcomes would not benefit from re-appraising play, so please recommend this book or buy a copy for friends, family, colleagues or employees.

I'm not just trying to drum up book sales (well, I am a little bit!), rather there is a benefit when everyone around you also understands and follows this approach.

When it comes to play, it's much easier to make changes when everyone is 'singing from the same song sheet', supporting each other's play rather than acting as each other's prison guard.

You could say I'm on a one-man mission, with individual clients, in my corporate workshops and consultancy work, to wake people up to the importance of play. It's one of the best investments any individual or organisation can make, so I'm passionate about helping people to understand and apply it more effectively.

Welcome to *The Play Paradigm!*

SNAP Approach

As a theme present throughout my work, I believe that approaches to personal development and self-help are most effective when they include the following qualities:

S – Simple
N – No Fluff or Filler
A – Accessible
P – Powerful

I am therefore committed to writing 'breakthrough books' that are usually well **under 100 pages in length,** and do not contain any unnecessary padding. The goal is to provide ideas and strategies for the reader to absorb and apply practically and rapidly.

<u>**It often only takes a *small* nudge or change to alter an individual's overall direction of travel, leading to *big* results!**</u>

As ever, I offer my ideas simply as MY opinion. You may take some things from this book that become YOUR truth, whilst others you may discard as you wish. As ever, make your own mind up and take what you need as you create your individual recipe for success and happiness.

Note: All case studies used in this book have had names and identifiable features changed to preserve confidentiality.

2.
THEORY

What Is Play?

Play is one of the 'Magic 3' segments of the Life Balance Wheel that I use in my therapeutic and coaching work – the others being Work and Leisure. (Note: We will look at the whole wheel later).

Why are these three so special? Well, from my clinical experience, issues and imbalances in these areas have the most impact on a person's ability to make and sustain positive changes.

More than just the specific activity, play is a transformational, balancing and nourishing state that promotes wellbeing. From my experience, it also has a lot in common with hypnotic states – focused attention, losing yourself in the moment, conscious mind and self-awareness subdued, subconscious mind stimulated and engaged, etc. All of these qualities sound pretty hypnotic to me!

Quickly defining the other areas, Work is usually the thing you are paid to do and Leisure includes activities outside of work, which may be enjoyable, but don't quite create the play state described above.

'I'm Not Sure I Get What Play Is?'

This is probably the response I receive most often when introducing this concept. The more genuinely unsure you are as to what play is, usually the more opportunity for positive growth you have, which is the good news.

Expanding on what I've said above, play is something you do which is pure 'me time,' pure focused attention and enjoyment, so much so that you lose sense of self, time, worries, cares and concerns. As we will explore further, play involves an almost child-like sense of absorption and joy.

I'm going to use the 's' word here – play is any such activity that is good for your SOUL. You feel better after, rested and more balanced. And you can't wait to do it again.

You don't have to learn play. You have to un-learn the denial of it.

Here's the great news – you already instinctively, intuitively know what play is and how to do it because you were born with the ability and impulse to play.

Just like how we are all born confident – think how a baby confidently demands attention - the nurturing or suppression of these qualities is something we LEARN.

Some of this learning occurs through our own direct experience, but much is through what we are taught by parents, family, teachers and other socio-cultural influences.

Play – From Hero to Zero

Whereas, a baby's natural confidence is put into check very early on to socialise and train the child, play actually *is* valued by society for a long time during childhood. There is consensus that children need to play, and they learn best through play.

This is the 'hero phase' of play. It's almost like we can't get enough of a good thing – schools and parks have a PLAYground, education features PLAYtime, time is allocated for us to visit friends and PLAY.

However, the clock is always ticking in this phase because at some point you learn…

PLAYTIME IS OVER!!!!!

Usually coinciding around the time of puberty, the rollercoaster of emotions and hormonal changes makes this a perfect time (sarcasm) to introduce another big change – PLAY is now a relatively dirty word.

'Can you stop PLAYING up?'

'You're PLAYING around at life - you need to decide what you are going to be and do!'

The Grown-up Rules

The new suggestion and paradigm we are sold by society and our caregivers at this point is usually a re-ordering of the priority and balance of the 'Magic 3' areas of Play, Work and Leisure.

Work now becomes the focus (obsession?), appropriate Leisure next (appropriate to whom?) and then finally Play gets whatever time and energy is left.

<u>WHAT A TURNAROUND?!!!!</u>

GUILT is also a new feature of the 'zero phase' of play - not only should play be the lowest priority, but if you take time / energy / resources from any other area of your life, you may be encouraged to feel guilt or shame.

'How can you be playing when you SHOULD be spending time on…?'

The result is, that at best, play is often minimised; at worst it is virtually eliminated.

The carrot dangled is that by working long and hard enough and by continuing to pay into that pension, one day you might get a chance to play again. If that was ever true, this model is arguably far more broken and defunct now.

Likewise, many people work flat out all year and then go on holiday for a couple of weeks. Trying to squeeze all of your play into such a short period of time creates that type of holiday where you spend about a week just getting over the stress you left behind and then about a week worrying about the stress awaiting you on your return (all those emails that will be building up!) You *might* get 1-2 days of play or 'holiday' in between. Awful.

This is what I refer to as the toxic, anti-play paradigm.

Here's the kicker – you WILL find play anyway, but not always the right type!

Because play *is* so hard-wired as a human need (not just humans either, look at an animal's instincts to play), even when we consciously deny ourselves play, subconsciously we will find a way to manifest it.

Healthy vs. Unhealthy Play

This is an aspect of my approach to play that emerged from my clinical work. Almost every time someone books a session for bad habits or addiction, when we do this analysis, it is clear that a lack of genuine healthy play is either a major part of the problem or a key factor as to why they haven't previously been able to sustain a positive change in direction.

In simple terms, with too little or no healthy play, a person can find it easy to pick up unhealthy forms of play which then become habitual and problematic.

However, it's not just bad habits that can thrive in an atmosphere of reduced play - low mood, stress and anxiety can all be symptoms.

<u>YES! Many of these PROBLEMS can be SYMPTOMS of an unhealthy relationship with play - change this and you can go a long way to improving or even eliminating them!</u>

However, the reverse is also true. If you don't establish a healthy relationship with play in your life, all the therapy, counselling or change work in the world won't be as effective as it could be, because it may be treating the symptom and NOT the problem.

This is part of what I call creating the right 'Foundation Mindset' for positive change. Without a firm foundation, the house you are building will either not progress very far or won't stand up for long before collapsing.

'But What Is Healthy Play?'

Healthy play is play that usually doesn't involve any recreational substances and where any habits formed are good for your mind and body.

That's not to say a person cannot enjoy occasional nights out drinking with friends, but rather understand that this should come from your leisure quota and not play.

The logic is simple - if the only occasions you are enjoying the pure 'me time' and escape of play is when drunk, that is clearly unhealthy and potentially a recipe for disaster.

CASE STUDY: Smoking Cigarettes as Instant Play

Sarah is a board level exec with high stress levels. She says that she lives a 'work hard, play hard' lifestyle. (This is always a red flag, as in reality, this is usually 'work hard, leisure hard plus unhealthy play'.)

She does sports and social activities, but these tend to be chosen by her husband or related to her kids. Despite the fact she clearly has leisure activities, under closer analysis, following *The Play Paradigm* it is clear her play is almost non-existent.

However, remember, we need play at a deeper level, so we will manifest it anyway. No surprise, Sarah then finds herself drawn to the unhealthy play of her smoking habit.

As the owner of a leading London smoking cessation clinic, I can tell you with authority that this is what smoking really is for many people - a habitual, unhealthy form of play or 'me time.'

Because Sarah has no healthy structured play, when her mind is crying out for 'me time,' she takes *her* play in relatively cheap, instant 'fixes' in the form of cigarette breaks.

Of course, Sarah still needs to break the habit (for example, using hypnotherapy as I provide), but to sustain this change it is also vital that she re-appraises and takes a fresh approach to expanding healthy play in her life.

Most positive change follows this pattern – it is supported by the right amount of healthy play or potentially sabotaged by the lack of it.

This why *The Play Paradigm* is so important and why, like most powerful ideas, when implemented practically it can literally transform your life.

Playtime may have felt like it was over, but it's beginning again NOW!

3.
FOUNDATION MINDSET

You may already be feeling a sense of nervousness or trepidation.

It may go something like this…

'Yes, that makes sense!!! BUT…'

Ah, those big 'buts' can really weigh us down. That's the negatively-programmed, socially conditioned part of your mind already becoming uneasy with the idea of investing in play (this term is important as play is genuinely an investment in your life).

Because the way we comprehend time leads us to view it as a finite resource, once we understand the Life Balance Wheel, we can jump too quickly, seeing it simply as a 'zero sum' game. If the pizza slice of play is bigger, surely something is being taken away from the other areas of a person's life.

Following this flawed logic, by expanding play, I could be telling you to:

- Be less diligent at work
- Neglect your family or children
- Ignore your friends

Again, this is underpinned by GUILT which I mentioned earlier - a creeping feeling that prioritising play is somehow selfish or just wrong.

IN FACT, THE OPPOSITE IS TRUE!!

This is what gives applying *The Play Paradigm* a counter-intuitive feel at times – how investing in play, even when we feel we shouldn't, actually brings about IMPROVEMENTS in other areas of life, such as work and relationships.

But why would this be? Surely, in terms of time, if you spend more on yourself, you spend less on everything else? In a strict sense this is true, but it ignores the key issue, which is QUALITY OF TIME.

Firstly, regardless of how busy a person is, they can always improve organisation, efficiency and 'find' more time if they really try.

Secondly, does making play a low priority REALLY benefit those other areas? When we personally don't get enough play, it actually has a negative impact, making them seem more like a chore and duty, and on some level often creating resentment.

CASE STUDY: A Fun(Less) Day at The Zoo

Steve had been working hard in his self-employed business and had a busy family life with two children. He had little time for leisure or play and although he used to play five-a-side soccer, he kind of fell out of it when his second child was born.

On paper, this is model citizenship - he is working hard, paying taxes, raising his family and putting their needs FIRST. There is no time for *his* play, because remember, what we are largely conditioned into believing is that adulthood means 'playtime is over'.

The weekend comes and Steve promises to take his kids to the zoo. Already the day starts badly, as he wakes up in a bad mood and it takes ages to get the kids out of the door. Finally, they set off, but they've forgotten something and have to turn back before setting off again. Steve snaps a couple of times and then apologises, explaining 'Daddy is stressed and wants us all to have a nice day.'

True to his word, Steve does TRY and have a nice day, but kids are pure intuition, they have a sixth sense for when someone is not really engaged. As a result, the day is okay, but not great. Steve feels shattered afterwards as well.

The problem now is that if Steve explores how he is feeling, the toxic anti-play paradigm can lead him to conclude he is a bad father. I mean, he took his kids to the zoo but wasn't really up for it. Oh my, does he RESENT his own children! Now he feels even worse!

Nope, Steve is not a bad father. He is A HUMAN BEING with his own play needs too. With these unmet, his ability to function in the other areas was impaired.

IGNORING PERSONAL PLAY TO FOCUS ON OTHER AREAS OF LIFE IS THE ILLUSION OF BEING FUNCTIONAL - WHEN YOU EXPAND HEALTHY PLAY YOU ACTUALLY BENEFIT THE OTHER AREAS OF YOUR LIFE!

This is the number one concept to understand, and whilst it takes a small leap of faith, the sooner you accept it, and apply it, the better.

The tiny amount of time taken away from an area of your life for play will pay 10 or 100 times returns in the change in quality of time in the other areas.

'Hang on, my work is really high-pressured. If I take my foot off the gas, I'll be in trouble!'

I hear this a lot and my reply is always a variation on:

'If you <u>don't</u> start investing in play you <u>will</u> be in trouble, if you are not already. Plus, have you ever considered that your work will be better, more productive and enjoyable if YOUR play needs were satisfied?'

See what I mean by the anti-play paradigm being toxic – as a society we start to almost fetishise the idea of working ourselves to burn-out or death. Endless talk of the 'grind' on social media just reinforces this unhealthy obsession.

It's great to work hard, but without play it's just another form of dysfunction. Eventually a person runs out of gas or picks up an unhealthy play habit that derails them or, ironically, impacts negatively on the very areas of their life they thought they were putting first.

4.
PRACTICAL GUIDANCE

Defining Play for YOU

It would be great if I could just write a list of activities for you to follow and Abracadabra! there is your play, but in reality play is highly personal and subjective.

One person's play can be another person's leisure or even work!

So, the first step is to take some time to REALLY think about what play means for you. You may already have some ideas, but even if you don't, what you are looking for is a healthy activity that includes the following qualities:

- Your needs / wants are the priority, i.e. 'me time'
- It captures your focus and attention
- It can lead to you losing track of time, sense of self, and even peripheral awareness
- It may feel childish or a 'guilty pleasure'
- It might be VERY different to your usual leisure activities
- It makes you happy and feel more balanced
- It makes you feel restored or recharged
- You feel better for doing it and want to do it again

I believe that play falls into the group of transformational states where the mind repairs and restores itself, similar to 'dream sleep' and hypnosis. The fact that it makes you feel great afterwards is a good marker of genuine play.

A simple way to identify *your* play is to look back in your life – what previously gave you the above mentioned feelings? It doesn't matter how far back you go, sometimes childhood pursuits provide a great starting point for play ideas.

The idea of play often feeling like a 'guilty pleasure' comes up again and again in my work and makes sense in the light of the socio-cultural programming I have already explained.

Typically, when I introduce these ideas, a person will initially say, *'I don't think I get any play.'* I will then describe the qualities above and ask them to recall a time when they did.

This is often a breakthrough moment. After a pause where they are filtering their response through the limiting beliefs about what play *should* be, they will often sheepishly suggest there *is* something but it's *'ridiculous'* or *'I can't do that, can I?'*

THIS IS ABSOUTELY THE FLASHPOINT MOMENT FOR CHANGE!

Provided it's healthy, legal and doesn't harm you or another person, whatever you are shy or sheepish about admitting is play to you, really is as valid as anything else.

So, stop judging your play! Your parents, social connections and even you, yourself, might like the *idea* that watching the opera is play to you, but if it doesn't tick the boxes above, at best it can only ever be leisure.

If bouncing on a trampoline or reading trashy romance novels produces the play state, then that's *your* play. Don't suppress it, but embrace it and, more importantly, actively make time for it.

CASE STUDY: 'You Can't Play Video Games at Our Age Though, Can You?'

Adam was a client with a very responsible job. He was struggling to think of what play meant to him, but was sure he wasn't getting enough of it.

After some time wracking his brain, I asked him about previous play in his life and he smiled and said, *'Well, I used to love gaming when I was a teenager.'* I asked him to describe the feeling and he explained how it would de-stress him, he would lose himself in it and it was just a fun part of his life when he was in college.

I asked Adam if he could explore the activity again and he gave the exact response in the title of this case study. The language he used was VERY telling, as it revealed his limiting belief around the appropriateness of the activity now.

Notice how he said YOU, OUR and YOU again and not 'I'. This is classic subconscious projection – revealing a belief that professional men in their mid-thirties shouldn't play video games whilst also seeking agreement from me as to the validity of this belief.

I replied, 'Oh, *personally,* I can play video games at any age, but what I want to understand better is precisely why YOU think YOU can't?'

What followed was the deconstruction of his limiting belief built on the idea that he was always told gaming was a 'waste of time' by his parents. This opinion had become his truth and reality, but once he understood *The Play Paradigm* he could make his own decision as to the value of the activity. He bought a new games console that afternoon.

Challenge Your Limiting Beliefs About Play

If you find yourself applying the words *shouldn't* and *can't* to the appropriateness of play, actively challenge these beliefs and deconstruct them.

Ask yourself:

- Where did the belief about this activity come from – does it reflect your best interests or someone else's (possibly ill-informed) opinion?

- What's the worst-case scenario if people discovered your 'guilty pleasure' form of play. Would your clients really leave you if they knew you were taking breakdancing lessons? Perhaps they would like you more.

- On the simplest level – why the hell not do it?! Life is not a rehearsal and play is so important to your wellbeing. Provided it is healthy play, pursue whatever works for you.

PEOPLE WHO GET ENOUGH PLAY ARE HAPPIER, MORE ATTRACTIVE AND HAVE A POSITIVE ENERGY ABOUT THEM – THIS ALONE OUTWEIGHS ANY PERCEIVED RISK FROM A FORM OF PLAY WHICH RAISES EYEBROWS AMONGST FRIENDS, COLLEAGUES OR CLIENTS.

'I really find that person miserable and emotionally-draining, but that's fine because they have exactly the same set of interests as me' said no one, ever.

ACTION STEP: List or Mindmap Ideas for Play

- Go somewhere different, i.e. not a place usually associated with work or another type of leisure, take out a blank piece of paper and just write intuitively.

- Start with the 'low-hanging fruit' of play you may already be doing or have enjoyed previously. Then move on to new ideas, things you have never tried or maybe even considered before.

- If you run out of ideas, stop, distract yourself with something different (listen to music, watch something) and then return to the list.

- Especially welcome 'crazy ideas' for possible play and embrace them with a 'why the hell not?' attitude. No one has to see this piece or paper, so let your imagination loose!

ACTION STEP: Analyse Where You Are Right Now

The next step is to perform an assessment of satisfaction levels across your life, including in the area of play (now you know what it is and isn't), by completing the Life Balance Wheel below.

This is the style of wheel I use in my **HD Coaching Method** and I find it a powerful tool for personal development.

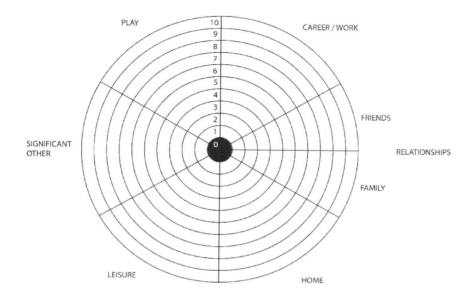

You can download a PDF copy of this to print out and use via my website at *https://rorymj.com/life-balance-wheel/*

Rate each section from 0-10 where 0 is completely unsatisfied and 10 is completely happy and satisfied, using a coloured pen to fill in the sections one by one.

As I mentioned, *The Play Paradigm* puts a special focus on the 'Magic 3' of Work / Play / Leisure, but all areas are worth analysing to better understand the balance across them.

Career / Work – Your job or work, how you feel about it both day-to-day and in terms of your longer-term career.

Relationships – Give a separate rating for Friends and Family, indicating how happy you are with each of these relationship types.

Home - This area refers to the space, wherever that may be, that you call 'home.' How comfortable and happy are you with that place? (not so much the relationships within it, as these are covered more in the Relationships section)

Leisure - This refers to the hobbies and interests that you pursue mostly away from work.

Significant Other - This can be a partner in the romantic or life sense, a best friend or even a family member. Put simply, it refers to the most important person in your life and how you feel about your relationship with them.

Play – As already explained, this section is different from leisure and refers to complete 'me time.' Things that you do for just for yourself and which have the qualities already explained.

Ideally, the shape of this wheel should allow it to 'roll' smoothly and it's a useful exercise for identifying not only how you feel about play but also how you feel about it in relation to those other areas. You will also be able to explore ways in which, by expanding play, you may be able to lift up low-scoring areas of your life.

For example, maybe you dislike your job and the rating for Career / Work is low because you have a poor work / play balance. If play is expanded, this may change your perspective and experience of the job, making it score higher in the future.

It is worth re-doing the Life Balance Wheel every six to eight weeks to monitor your progress and any changes in satisfaction levels.

Asking for Support for Your Play

At this point, you probably get the idea of how important play is (it always was, but the world possibly made you forget!) and have some (even if just a few) ideas on what more play could mean for you.

But how do you now make the time and what are other people going to think?!

When I say that play is pushed to the bottom of the priority pile because of socio-cultural factors, these also include many of the people around you – the ones you love, depend on, who depend on you and with whom you work. One way of looking at many of these people is that they are the 'stakeholders' in your life.

You may previously have asked your boss for a change in work hours so you could go to a fitness class and been told 'NO,' or asked a relative if they could take your kids for a few hours one night so you could just watch a box set and unwind, and also been delivered another big fat 'NO'.

Worse still, if the rebuttal came with a variation on *'You want me to give up MY time to help you prance around in the gym or watch TV like a coach potato, you must be joking!'* it would be no surprise if you now felt guarded or awkward about asking for help again.

BUT HERE IS THE DIFFERENCE - THIS TIME YOU ARE GOING TO DISCUSS THE IMPORTANCE OF PLAY FIRST, NOT JUST ASK FOR SUPPORT FOR SPECIFIC ACTIVITIES!

Remember how play is different for different people? Well, when you previously asked and got rejected, it's not necessarily because the person didn't want to help, rather they probably didn't know how important THAT activity was to YOU.

For example, watching a box set for four hours with your feet up might just be a pointless leisure activity to THEM, but for YOU it's the vital play time that reduces your stress, balances your emotions, calms your mind and improves all those other areas of your life (including your relationship with that other person).

They may also not fully understand the importance of play generally but that's easily solved, loan them or buy them a copy of this book. Failing that, bribe them with food and read it to them. Do whatever it takes, just make sure they get the concept of play.

When I work with companies and organisations, it is important that this fresh approach to play is applied 'root and branch', creating a network where we understand, respect and support each other's play - promoting a culture of play, if you like.

ACTION STEP: Start a Conversation About Play With Your 'Stakeholders'

- Start by explaining that you've been doing some work on your own personal development and you want to make some improvements.

- Explain the concept of play and if you are experiencing negative issues in your life draw a link to how a lack of play can both amplify and directly cause these.

- Ask them about THEIR experience of the play state (they might reply with, *'Oh, I get that feeling when I go for a long run'*, for example).

- <u>Explain how, with play expanded in your life, you will become better in the area they are most invested in (this is</u>

<u>true, as healthy play improves all other areas – better friend, better worker, better partner, better parent, etc.)</u>

- Start discussing YOUR ideas for play, drawing a parallel with their version of play. This helps the person better understand what you need. For example, *'You see, that feeling you get when you go running, well I get that when I'm learning a new magic trick.'*

- Agree practical ways that you can support each other's play.

Finding the Time for Play

You've now got some ideas for expanding play and maybe even some support to do it. So how do you now implement this new approach and turn it into a positive habit?

Notice how I say 'finding' the time and not making the time? The time you need is already there; you just need to release it so it can be redirected into play.

A typical starting point is to look at leisure activities which you might have previously thought were play, but don't provide the same state or benefits. In this case, changes are simple. For example, lose a gym session that is leisure and replace it with reading a novel in a coffee shop that is play.

Otherwise, look at the Life Balance Wheel areas which score lowest. Since you may already be unhappy with these areas, speak to the stakeholders in them about how investing in your personal play could make you function better in them.

As opposed to seeing the problem as how to divide your total time across each of these life areas, it is useful to reframe the challenge as one of planning and organisation.

An interesting observation from my clinical and coaching work is how highly organised a person can be in so many areas of their life and yet play is nearly always 'left to chance'.

This is another example of how little priority we traditionally put on play – it often receives the 'leftover' time in our adult lives.

There are nearly always ways you can introduce strategies and systems to streamline your life, boost efficiency and find the time for the play you need.

ACTION STEP: Ring Fence Play in Your Schedule

- The goal is to get organised and protective of your play time, so the first step is to get it into your diary or schedule.

- When planning your week or month ahead, whether using a paper or computer-based diary, try to block out play time as its own category of activity.

- This does NOT mean rigidly planning out every minute of specific play activities (where's the fun in that!) Just mark out the time for play and roughly put in some ideas of what it could be, still allowing you to be flexible and impulsive. The most important thing is that the time itself is being ring fenced.

- I recommend colour coding play in your diary, so that at a glance you can see how much is scheduled for a particular week or month and analyse any patterns that emerge. If you look back on a period where your happiness levels or productivity dipped, you can usually be sure that play was also neglected during that period and that its colour will be notably absent from the schedule.

Swapping Unhealthy Play for Healthy Play

As I have mentioned, expanding healthy play is a great way to help stay on track if you are breaking a bad habit or overcoming addiction.

In one sense, it is even easier to find the time for play in these situations since you already allocate both time and money to the unhealthy play.

In this way, you can look for 'swaps' for these type of play, specifically those activities that you acknowledge on some level could replace the need or impulse for the unhealthy play.

From my experience, most bad habits feel so ingrained because they have become so on a subconscious level. The human mind craves simplicity and favours automation of oft-repeated tasks, so it's no surprise that when the need or instinct to play emerges, a person opts for the easiest form of play, the unhealthy one. Instant gratification of the play impulse.

The problem, as we established, is that unhealthy play is, well, unhealthy! Usually the gratification is short-lived, the regret or shame sets in rapidly and then this continues the cycle leading to the next time.

For example, it's much easier after a long day at work, when feeling deprived of play, to pour a glass of wine (or two or three) than it is to arrange some other activity that might fulfil the same emotional need but in a healthy way.

The first step is to analyse WHAT emotional need the unhealthy play could also be satisfying.

ACTION STEP: Identify Healthy / Unhealthy Play Swaps

If you are looking to break a bad habit, this step can be very useful. If you don't have any bad habits, lucky you! You don't need this step, so you can skip it and read on.

Draw three columns on a piece of A4 paper as below – 'Unhealthy Play/Bad Habit, 'Emotional Need Satisfied' and lastly 'Possible Healthy Swaps.'

Unhealthy Play/Bad Habit	Emotional Need Satisfied	Possible Healthy Swaps

Now list those unwanted habits and really ask yourself what need they are satisfying in addition to the usual qualities of play. For example, do they relieve boredom, make you feel important, dispel feelings of loneliness or create a thrill or buzz? Then have a think about what healthy play activities could create the same or similar feeling.

It is the specific or 'straight swap' nature of this approach that can be so effective. You need to really drill into what the unhealthy play was giving you and then fill that need healthily.

This also explains why sometimes people who are trying to break a bad habit or overcome addiction struggle with play or new activities when prescribed by someone else.

For example, a person who has a cocaine habit where the need being satisfied is the buzz or thrill will not necessarily find a 'straight swap' in the form of yoga or pilates.

Those activities could be highly supportive, but they won't in this case necessarily be 'scratching the same itch' as the old behaviour. Plus, if the person doesn't really achieve the play state from the yoga or pilates either, they could be very useful and rewarding leisure activities, but still not genuine play.

However, maybe this person can think back to a time when they have had that rush of adrenaline or thrill feeling from a healthy activity. Perhaps they used to play squash and found the intensity and competition exhilarating. Maybe they could explore that again or something similar in intensity, such as boxing or martial arts.

It seems obvious when you think about it, but it's often a 'blind spot' for both people trying to make changes and those helping them. We can all too often project our own form of play onto others, assuming that's what THEY will benefit from too.

Therapists, coaches and other practitioners can at times be guilty of this. It comes from a positive intention – they are passionate about how effective a certain activity may be for an individual, but forget that it won't be useful or enjoyable for everyone.

For example, I am a big advocate of regular self-hypnosis using audios. I get great benefits from this personally and so do many of my clients worldwide. However, some people really don't take to listening to such audios. Sometimes I recommend meditation to them instead and they much prefer that, and vice-versa.

Now, as an experienced coach and therapist, I am flexible in my approach. But I guess that if all I knew was hypnosis, then hypnosis would be all I would be able to 'sell,' regardless of its suitability. If all you have is apples, then apples are what you are offering.

If you try to force any approach, technique or form of play on a person, you are trying to push a round peg into a square hole. It might stay in for a while, but after a short while it will spring out.

This highlights again the highly personalised nature of play and how important it is to define it correctly for the individual, so we can organise and also ask for what we need.

5.
STAYING ON TRACK

Once you have started to expand or have successfully expanded your play, the challenge is then ensuring that you don't slip back into old ways.

Diversifying Play

A great way to ensure you always have enough play is to maintain a variety of play options.

If you feel creative and get into the flow then it can be good to try some things that are completely new to you or that most people you know would be surprised you might try.

If you feel strapped for ideas of what new play could be why not ask someone else to surprise you with an activity and give that a go. You don't have to sign up for life, just go along, give it a try and if you find it is play (or could develop into play) then carry on exploring it. If not, move on. It's that simple.

When it comes to play the only real limit is your imagination.

Watch Out for The Unexpected Demand Snapback

This is the most common reason why a person rediscovers play and then seems to fall out of the positive habit of doing it again.

A sudden unexpected demand on your time and/or energy appears and that old programming kicks in - you look for somewhere to 'take' those resources from. What's the area of life that historically was afforded the lowest priority and the natural, knee-jerk one to borrow time and energy from? Play, of course.

This is an understandable but flawed response to an unexpected situation, so let's see how it can be avoided.

CASE STUDY: The False Economy of Raiding the Play Pot

Aisha had a job as an insurance executive and had spent some time reappraising and then expanding play in her life at the start of the year, coinciding with her turning 40. This involved making time for her passion of reading and also a regular language class where she was learning Spanish. Both of these activities were identified as play and her life and wellbeing improved massively by making time for them.

However, when a relative became sick, as the family member geographically nearest, she took on a lot of responsibilities for caring and checking in on that person.

Something had to give and it was play – both the reading and language lessons became sporadic and then eventually stopped altogether. Aisha's stress levels increased and her sleep became poorer. She felt bad even trying to make time for her 'stuff' when she 'should' be focusing not only on the sick relative, but her immediate family and work responsibilities.

In this instance the intention was well-meant, but the course of action was problematic and in the short, medium and long-term it will always create more problems than it solves.

**Remember, taking resources away from your PLAY is a 'false economy'!**

We NEED play and we will find it anyway and/or suffer a range of consequences. In Aisha's case her stress and insomnia increased, but it also created another negative knock-on effect (not dissimilar to the earlier 'zoo' case study).

Even though she was diligently looking after the relative and doing the 'right thing', her own lack of play and increased stress meant that sometimes she was grumpy and short-tempered with the person she was looking after.

This feeling of frustration and resentment made her feel a sense of guilt and shame (those old friends again!), which in turn meant that, more often than she liked, she was drinking a couple of glasses of wine in the evening just to 'feel better' and calm down.

Let's analyse this example so you can learn from it and make sure you don't make the same mistake in the future when facing a challenge.

Firstly, the expanded play was working well for Aisha, so it was irrational but understandable to diminish it when the new demand on her time and energy emerged.

However, she should have followed this simple rule:

If facing a challenge and you feel that play is the first thing you should reduce, it is probably, in reality, the LAST thing you should be reducing for your health, wellbeing and ability to face the challenge successfully.

It's all about perception and the framing of the demand. The rule that you 'should' put others first is misapplied when it comes to play and ultimately no one benefits.

What happened to Aisha? Once I was helping her, we worked on mindset, stress reduction and also looked at how her play could be restored again.

In practical terms, this meant speaking to those around her to get the support she needed to make time for her language lessons and reading. As is so often the case, once she REALLY explained and communicated her needs, most people were far more supportive than she had expected. She was able to re-establish her play and get back on track.

Oxygen Masks and Play

No, this isn't some kind of kinky detour I am taking you on. I am referring to being on a flight.

How often do we really listen to or observe the safety announcement before a flight? The cabin crew diligently perform their legal obligation to tell you what to do in an emergency, but we mostly just let this advice wash over us.

However, on a recent flight I thought of something that was a really good analogy for one aspect of play. My wireless headphones had run out of battery life (first world problems) and so I threw them down in a huff and found myself actually focused on the pre-flight safety guidance.

One thing stood out in a way that it never had before:

'In the unlikely event of a sudden loss of cabin pressure, oxygen masks will drop down from the panel above your head... Secure your own mask before helping others.'

__I snapped my fingers and thought, 'Wow, play is just like that!'__

The reason they have to tell you this instruction is because they know your HUMAN INSTINCT will often be to try and help others first, especially those you care about.

However, in reality, this instinct is risky to both your health and ability to ultimately help those around you.

You need to start seeing play in the same way. You really can't help others or functionally participate in the other areas of your life when your own play needs are not being met.

You might be able to struggle along, propped up by the unhealthy play you will most likely find anyway, but this will not be sustainable and is ultimately dysfunctional.

Even after this explanation, I have met some people who still hold the fixed mindset that leads to a reply of, *'Sorry, I don't agree. I always put others first.'* This could be an issue of ego or even just intelligence, but in terms of our individual play needs, it really is an illusion.

If this is you, I'd hate to be sitting next to you on a flight when I'm struggling to apply my oxygen mask and you've already passed out face first into your in-flight meal.

'Work Taints Everything'

This is an expression I use to explain the phenomenon of how work can creep into play activities and cause them to lose their core qualities and shift into a form of leisure or even just more work.

Work is always work. Regardless of how much you enjoy it or how fulfilling you find it, you will still need independent sources of play.

A red flag is when a person says something like, *'I love my work so much, it's not really like work. It's kind of all work and all play.'*

In truth, this is nearly always unhealthy and ultimately dysfunctional. From my clinical experience, I have seen a high proportion of people who hold this belief needing help with bad habits and unhealthy play.

This is because the play they THINK they are getting is really a work-play hybrid, which, if you follow the 'work taints everything' rule, only really has the qualities of work or leisure, but not true play.

For example, a person may be working solid five days a week, Monday to Friday, in their job as an engineer. On Saturday they play golf with some friends (they enjoy golf but it's not really play to them) and on Sunday they have a 'chill out day' to catch up on reading engineering books that have been on their reading list for a long time.

Can you see the problem? Five days of work, followed by a day of leisure and then a day of work masquerading as play. With the play day tainted by work, this person has gone seven days without any real play – bad for their wellbeing and far more likely to lead to unhealthy play if this pattern were to continue.

Monitoring the Evolution of Your Play

As time goes by it is wise to check that your play requirements are still being met by your scheduled activities. A quick check-up every six to eight weeks is usually sufficient.

A common issue is play becoming leisure, often slowly and unnoticed at first. This could be described as 'falling out of love' with a particular play activity – you might still like it, but you no longer love it, nor receive all of the wonderful benefits of true play.

However, there are other ways that an activity could stop being play, such as becoming work or being affected by a specific limiting belief or personality trait.

Case Study: Painting the Wrong Play Picture

Helen had an office job and painted in her spare time. The painting had originally been a rewarding form of play for her, so over the years she extended this to teaching art classes. She reported high stress levels that were prompting bad eating habits.

Upon analysis, it became clear that Helen was not getting enough play. The painting had been play at the start, but had literally become work so was no longer inducing the play state for her. She also said that she had a tendency to always 'try and make a business out of everything.'

I helped Helen to understand how this had led to her inadvertently sabotaging her play. I encouraged her to identify and explore new forms of play, whilst also making sure she was self-aware of the need to keep the play separate from work and her natural entrepreneurial tendencies.

When I caught up with Helen a year later, she was playing tennis regularly and taking a meditation class. She had quit the art teaching and 'felt much better for doing so.' After a break, she actually began painting again 'just for fun,' i.e. it had become play again. Occasionally, the thought had crossed her mind that she could train to teach meditation classes, but she is now wise to not act on that impulse. Every time she starts to think that way she consciously says to herself, *'This is play and I'm keeping it that way.'*

Play and Gratitude

A great way to stay on track with play is to make it part of your gratitude practice. If you don't practice gratitude as a technique, it's definitely worth starting. If you already do it, I recommend adding reflections related to play and the benefits of play.

Gratitude is a simple, yet powerful practice and many studies show a link to stress and anxiety reduction.

ACTION STEP: Practice Gratitude on a Daily Basis

The approach I recommend is to spend a few minutes before bed to physically write (as opposed to type) things that you are grateful for in your life, both large and small, that were part of your day. The effect is to focus your mind on positive thoughts and steer it away from negative thought patterns and cycles.

I recommend adding in specific items relating to play, expressing gratitude for your play, the benefits it brings, but also for those who support and help you to play.

Many people keep a dedicated gratitude journal for this purpose and this can be highly rewarding.

6.
LIVING PLAYFULLY

Once you start reaping the benefits of expanding play, you may wish to go even further in creating a more playful, play-centric life.

So far, I've really talked about the macro level of play, the big play activities that are so wonderfully important for your wellbeing. But there is also the micro level of play, small adjustments to everyday behaviour that could benefit from an infusion of play.

Now, here's the warning, some of this stuff can be pretty strange or wacky, but ask yourself a question - when you judge people for being playful and seemingly breaking social convention, are you really hating what they are doing or hating the fact you believe you don't have that playful spirit?

More often than not, if you are really being honest, it's the latter. The more vitriolic a person's judgement of someone else's play, the more frustrated they usually are with their own inability to be playful.

If there is an 'Inner Scrooge' lurking in your mindset, how about challenging that voice and experimenting with playfulness on as many levels as possible?

Playfulness and Mindfulness

If you have read my book *7-Day Mindfulness*, in it I explain how we can re-engage our five senses to help the mind spend more time in the present moment.

This brings a range of increasingly research-based benefits such as less time dwelling negatively in the past (a factor in some forms of depression) or the future (similarly a factor in some forms of anxiety).

I even talk about one of the key mindset qualities to adopt being 'New Born Curiosity,' but what is this if is not another way of describing playfulness?

Our everyday ability to be mindful is boosted by a spirit of playfulness when we are engaging our senses with the world around us.

Put simply, the more playful a person is, the more naturally everyday mindfulness comes and the more benefits they receive. If you needed any more reasons to make play a big part of your life, then this is another.

You can explore my straightforward approach to mindfulness at 7daymindfulness.com.

Playful Movement

When we think about how a child moves compared to how a very elderly person typically moves, the contrast is clear.

The child's movement are clearly energetic and fluid whereas the elderly person may be slower and more rigid. This contrast can be explained physically and biologically by the ageing process and its effects on the body.

But what about the still dramatic contrast between the movements of children and relatively young adults? Here, the difference is much more about socio-cultural programming and rules.

Children have a natural playful energy that leads to freedom of movement, skipping, twirling, jumping just for the hell of it.

However, as we grow up, once again this changes because of the rules we are given and the examples set by those around us.

Whereas once you could skip and dance anywhere, now there are rules - is there a dance floor and music playing? Are other people dancing? That's okay, you can dance. Are you shopping in a department store and feel like dancing a bit as you shop, since there is music playing? No, sorry that's against the 'rules' and inappropriate.

One again, consciously make a decision to question the basis, authority and usefulness of these 'rules'? Do they make your life better or worse? How could you begin to subvert them? Feels naughty, doesn't it? And great!

Now I'm not suggesting you immediately go from always following 'Don't Walk on the Grass' signs to suddenly performing the whole routine from Flashdance in your local supermarket. (If you do, take a photo / video and share with me!) Rather, start thinking about what physical movements throughout the day could incorporate more playfulness.

A great starting point is your morning routine. For many, this is performed with an atmosphere of grim solemnity. Since most of the activities are routine, they become pretty much subconsciously performed, carried out on autopilot.

For example, do you remember brushing your teeth in the morning, the Tuesday before last? There is a good chance that whilst you know you did it, you can't remember *that* time you did it SPECIFICALLY.

So, what could you do to make this part of your day more consciously playful? Maybe you could dance through your morning routine to different music or get ready in the manner of a famous celebrity or character (complete with impressions and mannerisms).

If you do the 'Are you talking to me?' scene from Taxi Driver, just make sure you do snap back into the real you before you leave for work. This is especially the case if you ARE a taxi driver!

Another idea is to look at your walk and how it links to your mood, perhaps you could you be more expressive and playful with how you stride, skip and step about your day.

Playful Language

If we rapidly get socialised into appropriately restrained movement, we certainly do so in our use of language.

We can become very formulaic and automatic in our language patterns and communication.

A starting point is to be more mindfully playful in small talk. When you start to analyse it, most small talk it is actually quite bizarrely automatic.

Person A: *'How are you?'*

Person B: *'Not too bad. You?'*

Person A: *'Yeah, could be worse, can't complain.'*

How many times have you heard this kind of conversation or even been a part of it yourself? Aside from the implicit negativity, person A is asking a question where there is an implicit expectation that Person B will not answer truthfully or authentically.

I remember once I was ordering a coffee in a local cafe and I did an autopilot, *'How are you?'* A quite charismatic and PLAYFUL barista replied, *'I was quite tired this morning, but, you know, the sun is shining and we've had lots of smiling customers like you, so I'm pretty good now, thank you! What would you like to drink?'*

WOW! That's honest and that's playful! Moreover, it made my coffee experience a thousand times better and I'm still sharing that story and that person's positive, playful energy now.

You could try using a different phrase when greeting people or experiment with calling someone you know by a new (non-offensive) nickname and seeing their reaction.

Don't stop at just being playful in the words you use. How about being more playful in your tone, volume, speech rate or in the gestures and facial expressions you use?

It doesn't really matter what you choose. The point is being aware that so much of your everyday communication will be formulaic and could really benefit from a conscious injection of play.

If you are delivering presentations or are in any type of client / customer-facing role, this playfulness can be really powerful. We have a natural, instinctive attraction to and curiosity of people and things that 'stand out' and being playful is a great start.

Have you ever noticed how a radio presenter that you seem drawn to listen to often has certain qualities in their speech? They change the pitch, volume and rate of speech just enough that it always sounds interesting and not just a flat, consistent monotone that would send people to sleep or cause them to 'tune out'. This often creates a playful tone that people find interesting and naturally warm to without even really knowing why.

Maybe deep down not only do we all need play, but also really do value it too.

Playful Environment

Could the spaces you live, work and spend time in benefit from being more conducive to playful interaction?

Have you got stuck in a certain way of organising your space at home? I'm a believer that when making big changes, it helps to make supportive smaller ones too. The latter often having a far greater effect on the subconscious mind than we think.

There can often be negative associations with a particular 'set up' in our environment. For example, perhaps you have spent many hours feeling down, eating junk food and watching the TV in the corner, slumped in your favourite chair. It's probably not a great idea when making positive changes to sit in exactly the same chair, in exactly the same way just minus the junk food. Often the subconscious mind will prompt or even compel the unwanted behaviours that had previously been performed in the old set-up.

The solution is to playfully mix things up – furniture positions, pictures, music, etc. – a fresh environment for a fresh mindset can work wonders.

7.
PLAY IN ORGANISATIONS

The concept of promoting play in the workplace and within organisations has gained traction in recent years. However, as I will explain, there are both good and bad ways for an organisation to approach play.

The key rule – you can't force a specific type of play on people!

I am often amazed when I advise companies and larger organisations how the advice of previous experts has all been so focused on prescriptive models of how to promote play in the workplace.

You can provide all the research-backed activities, toys and tools in the world, but they won't suit every individual. In fact, they often suit very few at all. This is why there can be a great deal of cynicism towards corporate attempts to promote play.

For example, having a ping-pong table might be a great idea for a company and some people will genuinely find it a fantastic form of play. However, others won't. Perhaps they hate ping-pong. Perhaps they hate anything competitive. But what they are sure to hate more, is being told they SHOULD play in that way.

Likewise, a teambuilding zombie escape game could be absolute play for some people, harmless leisure for others and, basically, for another group could actually feel like an extension of work.

'You WILL do this type of play and you WILL enjoy it!'

The real challenge with play in the workplace is that organisations are already swimming against the tide. As I explained earlier, 'work taints everything' when it comes to play, but note that I say 'taints' and not necessarily completely negates or destroys. There are still plenty of things an organisation can do to promote and benefit from play.

The first part of the solution is to understand that the teambuilding activities, the toys and games, might help people to be more playful during the working hours, but on a personal level they will be, at best, leisure most of the time.

If you want your employees or members to really benefit from play then you need to help them with the space, time and resources to experience it, whether inside or outside the workplace.

'Play Perks'

When I am helping organisations, the goal is to create a culture of play, usually by first re-educating their members on what play is (the essence of this book)!

Then we create a system of 'Play Perks,' some reward based, tailored to both the organisation and the individuals within in it. These can be time-based (e.g. an earlier finish to make a certain class outside of work) or vouchers representing a financial contribution towards certain activities, equipment or resources.

It absolutely remains true that a team should play together, but its members should also have the chance to play INDIVIDUALLY, and in a way that is right for them.

Some people need resources, some need time or rescheduling, but what is amazing with this holistic approach to play is how the whole team helps each other. Once everyone understands play, and values and respects each other's, they are happy to make the often small changes required to ensure that everyone gets their play.

This is not as complicated or expensive as some people worry it may be, and once again, a point I keep making is that when you invest in play, it pays a return in every other area. For example, a company usually sees staff retention rise, productivity increase and absence rates fall.

CASE STUDY: Sales Company Stop Selling Play

This company was really interesting. At first glance, they were a very modern, trendy company with a great culture. However, results, employee satisfaction surveys and retention rates proved otherwise. They had gone as far as creating a dedicated games room, adding in massage chairs and also organising regular group play activities for individual teams.

The problem was that all of this play was prescriptive. This is the illusion of a culture of play. Now, I have to reiterate all of these things they did were BRILLIANT for their staff, but were not so in the area of promoting personal play.

As most of their employees had high pressure roles and not enough play in their own lives, it was even more annoying when they were 'forced' to do certain activities in the name of play or to sit having lunch surrounded by the paraphernalia of play when deep down they felt they weren't getting THEIR play.

This might explain why people were frequently off sick when it came to group social activities or 'accidentally' stuck chewing gum into the workings of one of the massage chairs. There was also a fair amount of bathroom graffiti and magazine doodling / defacing - a sure sign of a frustrated play spirit, if ever I saw it!

The solution was an overhaul of the company's culture of play. I delivered workshops for the managers and also team members to ensure that, on a company-wide basis, everyone 'got' the concepts behind *The Play Paradigm*.

We also created a tailored system of Play Perks and built these in at a team level. In most cases, people needed either a little help with resources or time to achieve a form of play that worked for them.

We also made a few adjustments to the existing play space, splitting it between an 'activity' and 'chill out' zone. The latter included noise cancelling headphones, enabling people to either listen or read in peace, if that was a type of activity that suited them.

Where did all the time and money for this come from? It was simply reallocated – in broad terms, less spent on the generic forced play and more on helping people have the individual time and resource perks to engage in their personal play.

The result was a real culture of play where people were happier, worked better and, more importantly, felt listened to and valued. The biggest change was in staff retention. Who really wants to leave a company with a great culture unless they really have to!?

Integrating Play into Work Activities

With all the individuals in an organisation understanding and experiencing their own personal play, they will be far more receptive to other ways of integrating play into the working day.

Remember how I explained the socio-cultural programming that leads to our default attitude towards play and what represents 'normal' behaviour? Well, this is just as noticeable in the business world.

There are 'rules' and people follow them, often unconsciously and without question. How many companies and professionals look the same, act the same, sound the same, etc? This can make the world of work even more rule-bound in terms of social convention than our personal lives.

Professionalism does not have to mean being a dull, cookie-cut individual or organisation. You can be professional, deliver a great service, make money and have fun. These things are not mutually exclusive. It's just an unhelpful limiting belief if you think they are.

Here are some ideas for you, or the people who you work with or manage, to consider:

- **Eyes-Closed Breaks** – Many companies are catching on to the wellbeing and productivity boosting benefits of providing nap breaks. Some have even provided dedicated spaces, couches or 'sleep pods' for this purpose.

  However, I prefer the term 'Eyes-Closed Break' because it doesn't have to be sleep. It could be meditation or self-hypnosis (both easier when guided with an audio). You could check out my self-hypnosis and meditation MP3s at: *https://rorymj.com/mp3s/*

- **A Mindful Walk** – Don't chain yourself to the desk or computer, go out! A short walk on a break, paying mindful attention to your senses (what you are seeing, hearing, feeling, etc.) also the added bonus of providing exercise and a boost of Vitamin D.

- **Office Games** – From treasure hunts and quizzes, to puzzles and timed challenges, a quick Google search will produce hundreds of different games that can be incorporated into the working day and week.

  Try to have a balance of games that stimulate different qualities through play. Some are great for lifting the mood, others better for creativity.

  For example, I like the 'Laughter Game' for injecting some positivity and lightening the atmosphere. Seated in a circle, everyone takes a turn to solemnly say 'ha ha,' 'hee hee' or 'ho ho.' Anyone who actually starts laughing is eliminated and the winner is the last person left.

Once again, let your creativity loose and if you find yourself saying, *'Oh, I can't do THAT!'* there is every chance you are onto something promising in terms of play.

8.
FINAL WORDS

It is important to act on the information in this book, rather than just think about it.

A classic mistake is to put off making positive changes in mindset or personal development until a time when a person feels they will be 'less busy with work and life.'

This is the very thinking that can keep you trapped!

Instead, accept RIGHT NOW that play needs to become a priority and, even if it feels daring at times, at the very least for a few months make it an experiment to review the benefits as you make this change.

Once you truly understand and embrace play, you will feel like a veil has been lifted, a weight taken off your back and you will be able to live more authentically.

Playtime wasn't over, it was just suspended. The bell has rung, so go play!

41834600R00035

Printed in Poland
by Amazon Fulfillment
Poland Sp. z o.o., Wrocław